SO-ANP-628

GROWING NUTRITIOUS FOOD

Follow the Clues

by Tamra B. Orr

CHERRY LAKE PUBLISHING · ANN ARBOR, MICHIGAN

CHERRY
LAKE
Publishing

Published in the United States of America by Cherry Lake Publishing
Ann Arbor, Michigan
www.cherrylakepublishing.com

CONTENT EDITOR: Robert Wolffe, EdD, Professor of Teacher Education, Bradley University, Peoria, Illinois

PHOTO CREDITS: Cover and page 1, U.S. Department of Agriculture / tinyurl.com/ny7p4cu / CC-BY-20; page 4, © ZouZou/Shutterstock.com; pages 5, 7, and 24, © Monkey Business Images/Shutterstock.com; page 6, © Isuaneye/Shutterstock.com; page 8, U.S. Department of Agriculture; page 9, © Pressmaster/Shutterstock.com; page 10, © sanddebeautheil/Shutterstock.com; page 11, © Alexander Raths/Shutterstock.com; page 12, © Arena Photo UK/Shutterstock.com; page 13, © Spotmatik Ltd/Shutterstock.com; page 14, © Margaret M Stewart/Shutterstock.com; page 15, © photolinc/Shutterstock.com; page 16, © ifong/Shutterstock.com; page 17, © vivver/Shutterstock.com; page 18, © Lucian Coman/Shutterstock.com; page 19, © yuris/Shutterstock.com; page 20, © fotohunter/Shutterstock.com; page 21, © Naffarts/Shutterstock.com; page 23, © Elena Schweitzer/Shutterstock.com; page 25, © enzo4/Shutterstock.com; page 26, © Marina Lohrbach/Shutterstock.com; page 27, © phloen/Shutterstock.com; page 28, © Photographee.eu/Shutterstock.com; page 29, © Brent Hofacker/Shutterstock.com.

LIBRARY OF CONGRESS CATALOGING-IN-PUBLICATION DATA
Orr, Tamra. author.
 Growing nutritious food / by Tamra B. Orr.
  pages cm. — (Science explorer)
 Summary: "In this book, students see the scientific method at work in a real-world situation. Readers practice close reading as they look for clues that will lead to a deeper understanding of food, health, and the transfer of energy. The scientific method pushes students to apply critical thinking as they learn new methods of exploration and build on concepts they may already know. Additional tools, including a glossary and index, help students learn new vocabulary and locate information." — Provided by publisher.
 Audience: Grades 4 to 6.
 Includes bibliographical references and index.
 ISBN 978-1-63362-392-7 (lib. bdg.) — ISBN 978-1-63362-420-7 (pbk.) —
ISBN 978-1-63362-448-1 (pdf) — ISBN 978-1-63362-476-4 (e-book)
 1. Natural foods — Juvenile literature. 2. Nutrition — Juvenile literature. 3. Gardening — Juvenile literature. I. Title. II. Series: Science explorer.
 TX369.O77 2016
 631.5—dc23

2015015953

Cherry Lake Publishing would like to acknowledge
the work of the Partnership for 21st Century Skills.
Please visit www.p21.org for more information.

Printed in the United States of America, Corporate Graphics
July 2015

TABLE OF CONTENTS

CHAPTER 1

WHAT'S ON YOUR PLATE?

↑ Mr. Rowe knew the entire class would be eager to learn more about food.

Kai slid into his desk just as the morning bell rang. He grinned and waved to Tonya and Dylan, who were sitting two rows behind him. Kai's habit of rushing into class at the last minute never failed to make his two friends smile.

After taking attendance, Mr. Rowe stood up to introduce the day's lesson. "Today we are going to start learning about something we all know and love—food! We are going to discuss both healthy food and junk food. We'll talk about everything from familiar food you eat every day to exotic food you may have never heard of before."

Everyone began talking at once. The class was excited by the idea. Mr. Rowe smiled and gestured with his hand for the class to settle down.

"I've invited an expert to help us get started on this new topic," he continued, walking toward the door as he spoke. He opened it and poked his head outside. As he turned to go back toward his desk, a young woman followed behind him from the hallway. "This is Miss Gable, and she is a certified **nutritionist**," Mr. Rowe said. "She works for the local hospital and knows everything there is to know about food, so listen to her carefully."

Miss Gable chuckled. "Well, I'm not sure I know quite everything about food. However, I do know a lot about making healthy eating choices." She paused briefly. "What do you think the healthiest types of food are?"

Nutritionists might help plan the meals that students are served in school cafeterias.

"Hamburgers?" Jerome asked.

"Maybe pizza?" Teresa wondered.

"Ha! Wishful thinking," replied Miss Gable. "Those foods are fine once in a while, but they aren't healthy choices if you eat them every day."

"What about whole grain bread?" Dylan suggested.

"Or fruit like apples and bananas?" Tonya volunteered.

"Oh—and vegetables," Kai added. "My mom is always trying to get me to eat more carrots and broccoli."

"Your mom is smart," Miss Gable said. "Fruits and vegetables are full of **fiber** and **vitamins**, but low in **calories**. This means they are very healthy. Now, next question: how many of you have eaten fruits or vegetables today? And before you ask, ketchup does not count!"

Pizza can be delicious, but you shouldn't eat it too often.

Fresh fruits and vegetables are some of the healthiest—and tastiest—foods you can eat.

Only a few hands went up in the classroom.

"I'm not surprised," said Miss Gable. "Studies show that most young people don't eat enough fresh fruits and vegetables. You should be eating lots of them every day."

Mr. Rowe stepped forward. "This is an important problem," he said. "I want our class to brainstorm ideas for how we can eat healthier here at school. In fact, that is your assignment for tonight. Come to class tomorrow with some possible plans for ways we can all increase the amount of fruits and vegetables we eat each day."

Kai grinned and leaned back to whisper to Tonya and Dylan. "Now this is a project my mom will love!"

A HEALTHY PLATE

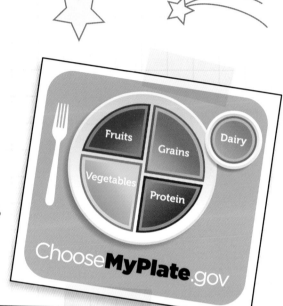

ChooseMyPlate.gov

The MyPlate program attempts to make it easy for people to choose the right foods.

One of the responsibilities of the U.S. Department of Agriculture (USDA) is to issue nutrition guides to help people around the country make better choices about what to eat. The first of these guides was created in 1916. Since then, the USDA's recommendations have undergone quite a few changes as scientists have learned more about food and nutrition. The current version of the guide was created in 2011. It is a simple chart shaped to look like a plate. This colorful image demonstrates the USDA's current recommendation for a healthy meal: equal amounts of fruit, vegetables, grains, and protein, along with a small amount of dairy. The idea is to make your own plate look like the MyPlate image for every meal. However, many experts believe that these guidelines could be improved. Nutrition is a complex subject, and eating healthy isn't always as simple as following a chart.

CHAPTER 2

BRAINSTORMING IDEAS

The class started out by writing down their ideas for improving their diets.

The next day, even Kai was in his seat on time when the bell rang for Mr. Rowe's class to begin. Tonya and Dylan exchanged a look of surprise.

"I hope everyone came up with some ways to improve our nutrition," Mr. Rowe said. "Take a minute to write your ideas down on small pieces of paper. Then you can pass around this box and drop them inside."

A few minutes later, the box was full of papers. Mr. Rowe pulled them out and listed them on the whiteboard one by one. The class spent a

lot of time weighing the pros and cons of each idea. Some were too easy—they would not make enough difference to notice a real change in diet. Others were far too complicated to complete in class.

Eventually, Mr. Rowe pulled an idea out of the box and said, "Hey! We might have a winner here!" The paper read:

We should plant a vegetable garden on the school grounds. Students would learn where food comes from and how to take care of a garden. Then, the food could be picked and served in the cafeteria.

Kai looked back at Tonya and Dylan. It was the idea they had come up with the night before as they walked home from their bus stop.

Growing a garden is a great way to make sure you always have plenty of fresh produce.

↖ Planting and maintaining a garden requires a variety of tools.

The room buzzed with conversation about the possibility of a school garden. What could be grown? Where would it go? Who would take care of it? Mr. Rowe promised to do some research that night and report back to them.

The next day, Mr. Rowe announced, "Well, guys, I think our school garden idea is going to work. I talked to Principal Wilson this morning, and she is all for it. She is going to look for a location where we can plant the garden. In the meantime, we have some hard work to do."

Everyone sat up straight. Did a school garden mean extra homework assignments?

"We need to find people in town who might be willing to donate supplies and advice," the teacher continued.

When planting a garden, you can purchase packets of seeds or start with partially grown plants.

"My Uncle George runs a plant nursery downtown," Letha said. "I'm sure he would help us pick out plants and seeds."

"I bet he could give us some great advice on watering, weeding, and all of that stuff," Connor added.

"My Grandma Sheila is a master gardener," Tonya volunteered. "I could ask her for some help, too."

"My neighbors own a small hardware store," Dylan said. "They might help us get shovels and any other tools we need."

"We should go to the school library and ask Mr. Hopkins about books on plants," Kai suggested. "You know, to find out what grows well around here, when it should be planted, and details like that."

Mr. Rowe smiled. There was nothing he liked better than seeing his class get excited about a new idea and run with it.

WHAT IS A NUTRITIONIST?

A nutritionist can offer advice to people who need special diets for health reasons.

Nutritionists are professional experts in nutrition—in other words, they know what makes some foods healthier than others. Some nutritionists provide diet advice to people who hire them. Others work at places that feed large groups of people, such as hospitals, retirement homes, and prisons. In addition to planning everyday meals, they create special diets for those with medical needs such as high blood pressure or diabetes.

Becoming a nutritionist requires a degree from a four-year university. Students who want to become nutritionists usually also complete an internship. This is a program in which they work alongside an experienced nutritionist to learn more about the field. Finally, nutritionists must usually pass an exam to earn a certificate and begin working on their own. It takes a lot to become a nutritionist, but it's an important job that requires knowledge to do correctly.

CHAPTER 3

SOIL AND SUNLIGHT

⤶ Soil must be prepared before planting seeds or plants in a garden.

"Mr. Rowe, when are we going to get started planting our garden?" Dylan asked.

The students were ready to move forward with their new project, but Mr. Rowe knew that they were several weeks away from putting plants in the ground. A space had to be selected and prepared for gardening, and the school administration had to finish the necessary paperwork.

"It is going to be a little while longer," the teacher admitted. "But," he said as the students began protesting, "that doesn't mean we can't get started here in the classroom. We are going to learn more about **photosynthesis** and how plants grow."

Mr. Rowe talked about the process of photosynthesis and how it allowed almost all plants and flowers to grow. He asked the class to gather around a table in the back of the room where several small plants were growing in pots. "Look at these plants we have and tell me what you notice," he said.

"They're all green," Kai suggested.

Most plants have green leaves.

Mr. Rowe laughed. "That's true, Kai. They're green because they are filled with **chlorophyll**. Chlorophyll is what makes it possible for the plant to absorb light from the sun and makes the sugars the plant needs to survive."

"But what about roots?" Dylan asked. "Don't plants absorb nutrients from the soil?"

"They sure do," Mr. Rowe replied.

"I'm confused," Kai said. "Do plants need nutrients from the soil *and* from photosynthesis?"

"Good question," Mr. Rowe answered. "Why don't we solve this one with a simple experiment. We'll use the scientific method to answer your question." He pointed at the scientific method chart hanging on the wall.

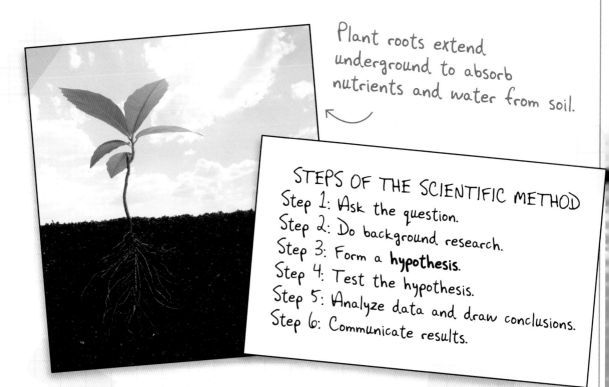

Plant roots extend underground to absorb nutrients and water from soil.

STEPS OF THE SCIENTIFIC METHOD
Step 1: Ask the question.
Step 2: Do background research.
Step 3: Form a **hypothesis**.
Step 4: Test the hypothesis.
Step 5: Analyze data and draw conclusions.
Step 6: Communicate results.

↳ A large window can provide plenty of sunlight for growing plants.

"So what is everyone's hypothesis? What will happen if we put some of these plants near the window and some of them in the closet?"

"I think the plants will be the same," Kai said. "The ones in the dark will just get their nutrients from the soil."

"I think the ones in the closet will start to die," Tonya said. "I'm pretty sure plants need sunlight to live."

"I think they'll both be fine," Dylan said. "But maybe the ones in the sun will grow faster."

The rest of the class contributed their hypotheses as they discussed the experiment excitedly. Following Mr. Rowe's instructions, they placed half of the plants near the classroom's big windows, where they could get

↖ Like people and other animals, plants need water to survive.

plenty of sunlight. Then they put the rest of the plants in the closet, where it was very dark.

"We'll make sure to water all of the plants equally and check on them every day," Mr. Rowe said. "As you check in on the plants, be sure to write down anything you notice about the way they look. Are they changing size or color? Do they look healthy? These kinds of questions will help you find out if your hypothesis was correct."

Over the next couple of weeks, the class kept careful watch over their plants. They took notes about everything they saw. As the plants in the sunlight continued to grow, the ones in the closet began to lose their green color. Their leaves sagged, and they looked unhealthy.

"Well," Dylan said, "I guess we've got an answer to our question."

"Yep," said Kai with a frown. "I guess plants need sunlight to make the sugars necessary for survival."

"No reason to be upset about it," Mr. Rowe said with a smile. "Experiments aren't about picking the right hypothesis. The important part is finding a solution to a problem or answering a question."

Kai's face brightened. "Well in that case, this experiment was a huge success!"

"It sure was," Mr. Rowe replied. "And the best part is we can move these healthy plants to our garden when it comes time to get started."

Potted plants can be transferred to the soil in a garden to continue growing.

A CLOSER LOOK AT PHOTOSYNTHESIS

Photosynthesis allows plants to harness the sun's energy to produce food.

The word photosynthesis comes from Greek words that mean "putting elements together with light." During photosynthesis, plants absorb energy from the sun. They combine this energy with water absorbed from the soil and carbon dioxide absorbed from the air. When these three substances meet, they react and produce glucose, a substance plants use as food. The reaction also creates oxygen, which the plant releases into the air. The scientific formula for this process looks like this:

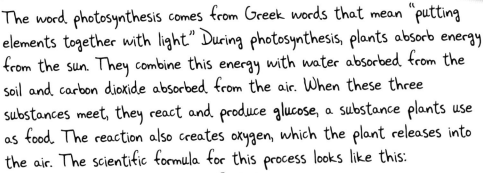

$$Carbon\ Dioxide_{(gas)} + Water \xrightarrow{Sunlight} Glucose + Oxygen_{(gas)}$$

   Because photosynthesis releases oxygen, it is also helpful to people and other animals that breathe air. Without it, we would not have healthy air to breathe. This means that growing a garden offers benefits beyond just improving our diets.

CHAPTER 4

PICKING OUT PLANTS

It is important to plan out a garden carefully rather than sticking plants anywhere they can fit.

Everyone in Mr. Rowe's class was working hard to decide what they should plant in their school garden. Should they include flowers or save all the room for things they could eat? Which plants grew the fastest, and which ones needed the most attention? Did some need more sunlight than others?

"What about some fruit trees?" Maria suggested. "Like apples or pears?"

"They would take way too long to grow and produce fruit," Tonya replied.

"Sunflowers are awesome. Let's grow some of those," Letha added.

"They are beautiful, but they don't produce as much food," Connor argued.

"Class," said Mr. Rowe as he walked toward the door and turned the knob. "I know everyone is trying to make good decisions about what to put in the garden. To help with that, Miss Gable has kindly agreed to come back and make some suggestions."

"Hey everyone," Miss Gable said as she entered. "I am so thrilled to hear about your school garden project. What a great way to learn more about how food is grown and see photosynthesis in action. Making choices about what to plant can be hard, though, so let's see if I can help. You will need plants that grow quickly and don't require too much extra work. Of course, they should also be things you want to eat when the cafeteria workers put them on the menu."

By the end of the class, everyone had agreed on what to put in the garden. As Miss Gable had suggested, each plant would grow quickly and easily and could be added to many different recipes.

Mr. Rowe drew a picture of the garden plot on the whiteboard. "This section will be used to grow spinach," he said. "It grows fast and can be picked and replanted every three weeks or so. Spinach can be eaten raw in sandwiches or salads, added to soups, or just steamed. It is high in iron and vitamins A and C. Over here," he continued, "we will plant carrots and radishes. Both are easy to grow and can be

Herbs are a healthy way to add flavor to your food.

eaten raw or cooked. And here," he added, "will be the herb garden, where we will plant some mint and basil." The class had learned how herbs can help improve the taste of food, and they were eager to try growing some.

Just then, there was a knock on the classroom door. A student handed a note to Mr. Rowe. He read it to himself and then grinned. "Perfect timing," he said. "We have the official go-ahead from the school to start our garden. Let the planting begin!"

COMMUNITY GARDENS

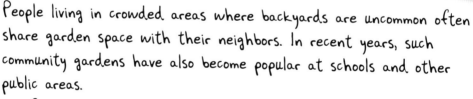

Members of a community garden might share supplies or help each other care for plants. ↳

People living in crowded areas where backyards are uncommon often share garden space with their neighbors. In recent years, such community gardens have also become popular at schools and other public areas.

Community gardens have many benefits. They give neighbors the chance to get to know each other and work together as a team. They provide healthy food while teaching young people where food comes from and how to take care of different types of plants. They also make neighborhoods more beautiful and release more oxygen into the air.

Many organizations offer money and other resources to schools that add gardens to their grounds. These programs make it easier for more and more schools to enjoy the benefits of a community garden.

CHAPTER 5

LESSONS FROM THE GARDEN

Vegetables and herbs can be combined to create soups and many other delicious dishes.

The cafeteria buzzed with the sound of student voices. Lunch hour had started, and today's meal was special. It was the first one to include some of the vegetables and herbs from the school garden. The cooks had included all of them in a tasty-looking soup.

As Tonya took her first bite, she said, "I can't believe I just picked these basil leaves this morning!"

"I know," agreed Dylan, looking into his bowl. "I'm pretty sure I recognize some of these carrots."

"These past few months have been a lot more work than I expected," Kai said about the garden. "But it has also been fun. Isn't it amazing how those tiny seeds grew into something we're eating for lunch? And guess what? I told my mom about the garden, and now she is growing herbs on our apartment's windowsill. This morning, I picked a fresh mint leaf and ate it. It was really good."

Tonya nodded. "My dad had kept a garden for years and then let it go. This past weekend, I helped him pull weeds, clear out rocks, and mix **compost** into the soil. Then we planted some tomato and cucumber plants."

Composting can turn old food scraps into nutrient-rich material that helps plants grow.

Radishes taste great in salads or on their own.

That afternoon Mr. Rowe's class shared a snack of radishes with dip made using the garden's herbs.

"Let's review what we've learned from this project," Mr. Rowe suggested. "First, we brainstormed ways to add more fruits and vegetables to our daily diets. We did some research and decided that a school garden could be a great choice. We experimented to learn how plants use photosynthesis, and then we finally grew some great veggies and herbs. So, how has the project helped you change the way you eat?"

"The spinach we grew was the first I ever tasted," Katherine admitted. "I thought I would hate it, but I didn't. In fact, I really liked it!"

↳ Carrots taste great raw, and it is easy to pack them in a lunch container with other tasty foods.

"I asked my mom to get me some carrots and dip for my sack lunches," Dylan said.

"My mom didn't have to remind me to eat my vegetables a single time over the past two weeks," Kai added.

"In other words, growing this garden helped to make cafeteria food healthier, introduced some new foods to you, and inspired you to eat more vegetables than you did in the past," Mr. Rowe said. "I can't wait to share these results with the school board! In the meantime, I declare this project a complete—and tasty—success."

EASY HEALTHY RECIPES

Veggies and dip is the perfect snack!

One of the best parts of having a garden is putting the healthy food you grow to good use in tasty recipes. One of the easiest snacks to make is veggies and dip. Start by choosing some of your favorite garden vegetables, such as carrots, radishes, or cucumbers. Have an adult help you cut the veggies into bite-sized pieces. You can make a simple, healthy dip by chopping up herbs such as basil or mint and mixing them with yogurt.

Another easy way to prepare garden veggies is to steam them lightly and then add a small amount of butter and parmesan cheese. This recipe works especially well with broccoli, carrots, cauliflower, or spinach leaves. Be sure to ask an adult to help when using a stove to steam your veggies.

GLOSSARY

calories (KAL-uh-reez) measurements of the amount of energy contained in food

chlorophyll (KLOR-uh-fil) the green substance in plants that uses light to manufacture food from carbon dioxide and water

compost (KAHM-pohst) a mixture of organic material, such as rotted leaves, vegetables, or manure, that is added to soil to make it more productive

fiber (FYE-bur) a part of fruits, vegetables, and grains that passes through the body but is not digested; fiber helps food move through the intestines

glucose (GLOO-kose) a naturally produced sugar in plants and in the blood of animals; it is a source of energy for living things

hypothesis (hye-PAH-thi-sis) an idea that could explain how something works but that has to be tested through experiments to be proven right

nutritionist (noo-TRISH-uh-nist) an expert in the science behind food and nutrition

photosynthesis (foh-toh-SIN-thi-sis) a chemical process by which green plants and some other organisms make their food

vitamins (VYE-tuh-minz) substances found in food that are essential for good health and nutrition

BOOKS

Bang, Molly. *Living Sunlight: How Plants Bring the Earth to Life*. New York: Blue Sky Press, 2009.

Gregory, Josh. *Composting at School*. Ann Arbor, MI: Cherry Lake Publishing, 2015.

Hengel, Katherine. *Garden to Table: A Kid's Guide to Planting, Growing, and Preparing Food*. Minneapolis: Scarletta Junior Readers, 2014.

Latham, Donna. *Respiration and Photosynthesis*. Chicago: Raintree, 2008.

WEB SITES

KidsGardening.org

www.kidsgardening.org

Check out this site for fun gardening tips and activities you can try at home.

Let's Move—School Gardening Checklist

www.letsmove.gov/school-garden-checklist

Find out more about school gardens from the U.S. government's Let's Move program.

School Garden Wizard

www.schoolgardenwizard.org

Learn how to work with your classmates and teachers to start a garden at your school.

INDEX

ABOUT THE AUTHOR

Tamra Orr is an author living in the Pacific Northwest. Orr has a degree in secondary education and English from Ball State University. She is the mother of four and the author of hundreds of books for readers of all ages. When she isn't writing or reading books, she is writing letters to friends all over the world. Although fascinated by all aspects of science, most of her current scientific method skills are put to use tracking down lost socks, missing keys, and overdue library books.